BAOBAB

AND MORE OF THE WORLD'S MOST AMAZING PLANTS

TOM JACKSON

Lerner Publications ◆ Minneapolis

Lerner Publications Company
An imprint of Lerner Publishing Group, Inc.
241 First Avenue North
Minneapolis, MN 55401 USA

For reading levels and more information, look up this title at www.lernerbooks.com.

Main body text set in Aptifer Sans LT Pro 14/18.
Typeface provided by Linotype.

Library of Congress Cataloging-in-Publication Data

Names: Jackson, Tom, 1972–author.
Title: Baobab and more of the world's most amazing plants / Tom Jackson.
Description: Minneapolis : Lerner Publications, [2024] | Series: Ultimate adventure guides |
    Includes bibliographical references and index. | Audience: Ages 8–11 | Audience: Grades 4–6 |Summary:
    "Explore Earth's weirdest forests, flowers that stink, and plants that kill in this engaging text. Full-
    color photographs and traveler's checklists bring the reader on an exciting journey through the world
    of amazing plants"—Provided by publisher.
Identifiers: LCCN 2023015970 (print) | LCCN 2023015971 (ebook) | ISBN 9798765609224
    (library binding) | ISBN 9798765625095 (paperback) | ISBN 9798765618660 (epub)
Subjects: LCSH: Plants—Juvenile literature.
Classification: LCC QK49 .J245 2024 (print) | LCC QK49 (ebook) | DDC 581—dc23/eng/20230620

LC record available at https://lccn.loc.gov/2023015970
LC ebook record available at https://lccn.loc.gov/2023015971

Manufactured in the United States of America
1 – CG – 12/15/23

Table of Contents

Chapter 1

FANTASTIC FORESTS

Forests are filled with trees, the planet's biggest plants. Trees grow tall to catch the sunlight and sink roots into the ground to collect water. But not all trees, or forests, are alike. Check out these amazing plants that create the world's weirdest forests.

Baobab Tree, Africa

Found growing in the dry parts of Africa, the baobab looks unlike any other tree. Its trunk is very thick compared to its branches, which appear to be too small. It is almost as if the tree has been uprooted and replanted upside down!

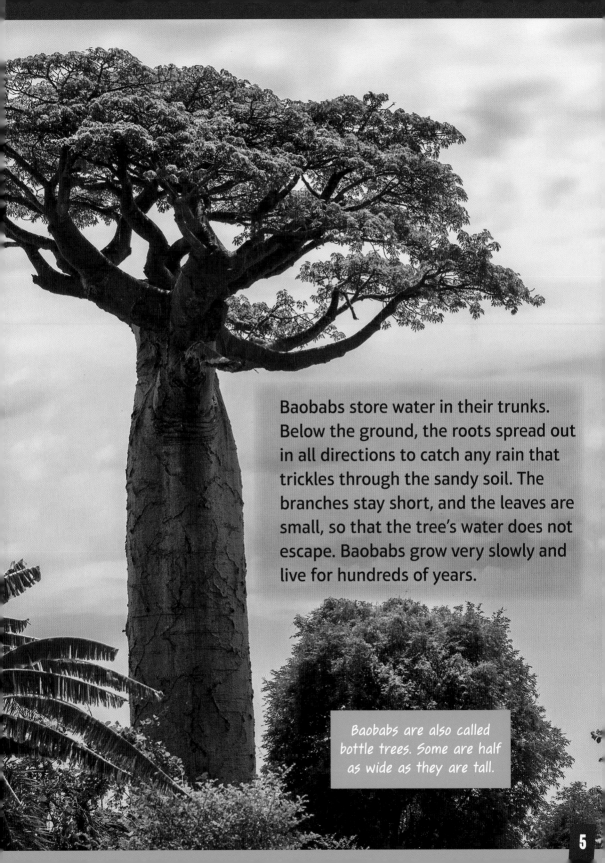

Baobabs store water in their trunks. Below the ground, the roots spread out in all directions to catch any rain that trickles through the sandy soil. The branches stay short, and the leaves are small, so that the tree's water does not escape. Baobabs grow very slowly and live for hundreds of years.

Baobabs are also called bottle trees. Some are half as wide as they are tall.

Pando, Rocky Mountains

In fall, this plant turns the hillside of the Rocky Mountains a beautiful yellow-gold color. These trees are better known as quaking aspens. This is because the trees' leaves tremble, or quake, when the wind blows through the forest. Quaking aspen trees do not always grow from a seed. Instead, they sprout up from the roots of a nearby tree.

Pando's leaves are green in summer, but they turn golden and fall off before the winter hits.

Many quaking aspen groves are actually all one plant. The trees are all connected together underground. The largest aspen grove of all is in Utah. It is a forest with forty-seven thousand trees, but they all make up just one plant, named Pando. Pando has been alive for eighty thousand years. All of its trees combined weigh as much as one thousand elephants. That makes Pando the heaviest living thing on Earth.

Rainbow Gum, Southeast Asia

Most forests are green, but these gum trees in the jungles of New Guinea and Indonesia show all the colors of the rainbow! Gum trees are also called eucalyptus trees. They have oily leaves with a distinctive smell. The gum tree's wood and bark are oily too, and as the bark dries out, slivers flake off. The fresh bark underneath meets the air for the first time and changes color, turning red, yellow, blue, purple, and pink. The color of a patch depends on how old it is, so each trunk shows many shades all at once.

The smooth bark looks like it has been painted.

Traveler's Checklist ✓

✓ **Wear a raincoat.** Rainbow gums grow in jungles where it rains every day, and a lot of water drips down from the treetops.

✓ **Wear hiking shoes.** There are no roads in the jungle. You will need to walk a long way to find the trees.

✓ **Pack food and water.** There are no stores in the area. Take everything you need with you.

Rainbow gum trees are tall. They can grow up to 250 feet (76 m) which is as high as a twenty-story building!

Giant Kelp, Pacific Ocean

There are forests along the coast of the northern Pacific Ocean, but you will have to go underwater to see them. This forest does not have any trees. Instead, it is made from a seaweed called giant kelp, which grows up from the seafloor. Sea lions head into the forest to hide from sharks. The killer fish cannot swim well among all that seaweed.

This kelp is the fastest-growing plant in the world. It grows 12 inches (30 cm) in just one day!

HOW SEA OTTERS PROTECT THE FOREST

Sea otters collect food in the giant kelp forest. They swim down to the bottom and collect tasty shellfish. These shellfish eat the kelp stems which kills the seaweed. The otters make sure the number of shellfish stays low so that plenty of kelp can keep growing. Without the sea otters, the kelp forest would disappear!

Chapter 2

KILLER PLANTS

Some plants eat animals! This is very unusual. Most plants get the food they need from sunlight and soil. But when plants can't do that, they must kill instead! Don't worry, these plants won't attack you!

Sundew, Venezuela

These plants grow in swamps or on damp, rocky hills. There are not enough nutrients in the soil here for many plants to survive. Sundews stay alive by getting the missing nutrients they need from insects. Sundews have hair-like spikes on their fleshy leaves. The spikes have droplets of clear sap on their tips.

This liquid is a deadly mixture of sugar and glue. Little insects perch on the plant to eat the sugar but get stuck! The leaves roll up to trap the bug. Over the next few weeks, chemicals in the sap turn the insect to mush, and the sundew takes in the useful nutrients.

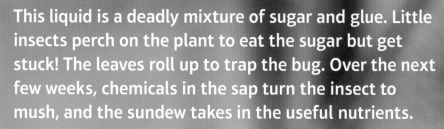

The sticky droplets catch the sunlight.

Sundews grow on the rocky table-top mountains of Venezuela where there is hardly any soil.

Pitcher Plant, Southeast Asia

These jungle plants have leaves that curl into a funnel-shaped cup—or pitcher. The leafy pitcher is filled with a liquid that gives out a sweet smell. Insects think the pitcher is full of nectar, a sugary liquid made by flowers. However, once inside, the animals cannot get out again. They are trapped by sticky goo, or they fall from the smooth walls and drown.

The pitcher has a lid to stop rainwater from getting inside. Big pitcher plants can trap lizards and mice!

Each Venus flytrap plant has several spiked traps.

Venus Flytrap, North and South Carolina

This little plant is one of the most famous in the world because of the way its leaves snap shut around flies and other insects. Venus flytraps live in the swampy forests of North and South Carolina.

The ends of a Venus flytrap split into two rounded sections called lobes. The lobes are connected by a hinge, and they have spikes around the edge that look like eyelashes. Insects land on the lobes to drink the nectar, and then snap! The lobes slam together trapping the bugs inside. The spikes along the edge stop the animals from wriggling free. Chemicals then turn the insect into mush.

This fly does not know what is about to happen!

Traveler's Checklist ☑

☑ **Don't touch.** The lobes of a Venus flytrap only work a few times before dying.

☑ **Walk carefully.** The plants are only a few inches tall and are easy to squash.

☑ **Visit in the summer.** The plants often die out in winter and sprout again in spring.

HOW DOES A VENUS FLYTRAP SNAP CLOSED?

The flat surface of a Venus flytrap is covered in tiny levers that look like hairs. When insects land on the trap, they will bend a few of these levers. The levers send an electrical signal to the rest of the lobe. The signal tells the lobes to push out some water. That makes the lobes floppier, and the stiff hinge then makes them slam together. It takes about five days to eat the bug, and then the lobes open again.

Chapter 3

FLOWER POWERS

The job of a flower is to attract attention. It is common for flowers to smell great and look even better thanks to their bright colors and petal shapes. However, these flowers attract attention in unusual ways.

Queen of the Andes, Andes Mountains

This rare plant is a distant relative of the pineapple. It only lives high in the Andes Mountains of Peru and Bolivia. It grows very slowly but lives a long time. By the age of one hundred, it can be 50 feet (15 m) tall.

The plant's long leaves look like a spiky ball.

Only when it is about a century old will the plant grow flowers. It makes up for lost time by producing the most flowers in the world! In just a few weeks, the whole stem is covered in thousands of flowers. Hummingbirds come to drink the nectar.

Stinking Corpse Lily, Indonesia

This is the world's largest flower. It is 3 feet (90 cm) wide and smells like rotting meat! The flower is made by a strange plant that grows underground and has no leaves. Instead of using leaves to soak up sunlight, this plant steals food and water from other jungle plants. Its huge flowers attract beetles that normally eat dead animals. These bugs move pollen between flowers so that the plant can make seeds.

The giant flower takes months to grow but only opens for a few days.

A Gemsbok antelope has come to graze on the desert flowers.

Namaqualand, South Africa and Namibia

For most of the year, this area of southern Africa is a sandy desert. However, it rains in spring, and the plants race to sprout before the water runs out. For a few weeks, the ground is covered in orange, yellow, pink, and purple daisies as far as the eye can see.

Chapter 4

STRANGE BUT TRUE

The amazing plants in this chapter do things very differently. Their strange way of life allows them to stand out from the crowd.

Living Stone, South Africa

It is hard to spot these plants among the sand and stones of the South African desert. Most of the time, they look like little pebbles.

A closer look at the strange plant shows that its rock-like body is made up of two rounded sections joined together. These lumps are actually fleshy leaves, which store water. They are small, at only about half an inch (1.5 cm) wide.

The living stones produce little flowers in the fall.

Being small stops the living stones from drying out in the hot sunshine. At dawn, the deserts are often filled with mist and fog, so the plants absorb these tiny droplets of water from the air.

Living stones grow a new pair of leaves every winter.

It is hard to see why, but the tumboa is a distant relative of pine trees.

Tumboa, Namibia

There is no other plant like the tumboa. It is perhaps the ugliest plant on the planet. With its ragged, browning leaves, it looks like it is dead most of the time. However, this plant lives in the Namib Desert, one of the driest places on Earth. It can survive for two thousand years.

The tumboa only has two leaves. The leaves are 4 feet (120 cm) wide and they can grow very long. As they grow, the tips of the leaves dry out and split into dead strips. The strips gradually break off. Each leaf can grow as long as 20 feet (6 m), but most of it is already dead. The plant has one thick root that plunges into the ground to collect the water deep down.

Ghost Mushroom, Australia

This mushroom is a type of fungus, not a plant. A fungus does not grow leaves or make its food using sunlight. Instead, it grows on its food, slowly turning it to mush.

The ghost mushroom lives in the forests of southern Australia. It eats dead wood and most of the year it grows thin, wispy threads that are hard to see. However, on rainy fall days, the fungus sprouts mushrooms from the dead logs. As night falls, the mushrooms start to glow green. In the dark, this light gives the forest a ghostly glow.

The mushrooms glow as chemicals inside them mix with the air. The younger ones are the brightest.

Traveler's Checklist ☑

☑ **Wear a raincoat and rain boots.** The ground and trees will be wet.

☑ **No flashlights.** The glowing is easier to see if your eyes are used to the dark.

☑ **Wait for a new moon.** It is best to visit on the darkest nights.

WHERE IN THE WORLD?

NORTH AMERICA

Pando,
Rocky Mountains

Giant Kelp,
North Pacific Ocean

Venus Flytrap,
North and South Carolina

Atlantic Ocean

Sundew,
Venezuela

SOUTH AMERICA

Queen of the Andes,
Andes Mountains

Pacific Ocean

Arctic Ocean

UROPE

ASIA

Pacific Ocean

Baobab Tree,
Africa

AFRICA

Rainbow Gum,
Southeast Asia

Stinking Corpse Lily,
Indonesia

Pitcher Plant,
Southeast Asia

Tumboa,
Namib Desert

Living Stones,
South Africa

Indian Ocean

AUSTRALIA

Namaqualand,
Namibia, South Africa

Ghost Mushrooms,
South Australia

Southern Ocean

Glossary

fungus: a life form that grows over its food; a fungus often grows mushrooms when it is time to breed and spread

grove: a group of trees

hinge: a link between two objects that lets them swing apart and back together

lever: a simple machine for pushing and lifting

lobe: a rounded body part

nectar: a sweet liquid that plants produce, often inside flowers

nutrient: a useful substance in food that living things need to survive

pollen: tiny, dust-like balls that plants use during breeding; to make new seeds, pollen from one flower is moved to another by the wind or by animals visiting to drink the nectar

sap: the liquid made inside a plant

Learn More

Active Wild: Weird Plants
   https://www.activewild.com/weird-plants

Baliga, Vikram. *Plants to the Rescue!: The Plants, Trees, and Fungi That are Solving Some of the World's Biggest Problems.* New York: Neon Squid, 2023.

Kaiser, Brianna. *Weird Plants*. Minneapolis: Lerner Publications, 2024.

National Geographic Kids: Lifecycle of a Flowering Plant
   https://www.natgeokids.com/uk/discover/science/nature/the-life-cycle-of-flowering-plants

One Tree Planted: Amazing Trees
   https://onetreeplanted.org/blogs/stories/amazing-trees

Ruby, Rex. *Gotcha!: Meat-Eating Plants*. Minneapolis: Bearport Publishing Company, 2024.

Index

Photo Acknowledgments

Image credits: lakkana savaksuriyawong/Shutterstock.com, p. 1; Dudarev Mikhail/Shutterstock.com, p. 5; Rafael Novais/Shutterstock.com, pp. 6-7; A. Michael Brown/Shutterstock.com, p. 8a; Lars Poyansky/Shutterstock.com, pp. 8b, 16b, 27b; Sabelskaya/Shutterstock.com, p. 8c; Larry-Rain/Shutterstock.com, p. 8d; Bill Florence/Shutterstock.com, p. 9; Ethan Daniels/Shutterstock.com, p. 10; David A Litman/Shutterstock.com, p. 11; Jolanda Aalbers/Shutterstock.com, p. 13a; Curioso.Photography/Shutterstock.com, p. 13b; Hamzi_faiz/Shutterstock.com, p. 14a; JTKP/Shutterstock.com, p. 14b; Dave Carroll/Shutterstock.com, p. 15; Linas T/Shutterstock.com, p. 16a; Blan-k/Shutterstock.com, p. 16c; ahmad agung wijayanto/Shutterstock.com, p. 16d; Matthias Kestel/Shutterstock.com, p. 19a; Christian Vinces/Shutterstock.com, p. 19b; Saichol Campan/Shutterstock.com, p. 20; Grobler du Preez/Shutterstock.com, p. 21; jgeyser/Shutterstock.com, p. 23; Navamin/Shutterstock.com, p. 24; Jef Wodniack/Shutterstock.com, p. 25; Petar B photography/Shutterstock.com, pp. 26-27; Anne Powell/Shutterstock.com, pp. 27a; olllikeballoon/Shutterstock.com, p. 27c; Andrei Minsk/Shutterstock.com, pp. 28-29; Cover: KENTA SUDO/Shutterstock.com.